indoor
water gardens

indoor
water gardens

Philip Swindells

Interpet Publishing

Published by Interpet Publishing,
Vincent Lane, Dorking,
Surrey RH4 3YX, England

ISBN 1-903098-49-1

Editor: Philip de Ste. Croix
Designer: Philip Clucas MSIAD
Studio photography: Neil Sutherland
Production management: Consortium,
    Poslingford, Suffolk
Print production: Leefung-Asco Printers
    Ltd,China.
Printed and bound in China

THE AUTHOR
Philip Swindells is a water gardening specialist with
a long experience of growing aquatic plants in many
parts of the world. He trained at the University of
Cambridge Botanic Garden and the famous aquatic
nursery of Perrys of Enfield, and ultimately became
Curator of Harlow Carr Botanical Gardens, Harrogate.
The author of many publications on water gardening,
Philip was also formerly the editor of the *Water Garden
Journal* of the International Waterlily Society who in
1994 inducted him into their Hall of Fame.

Acknowledgements
The publishers would like to thank the
following people for their help during the
preparation of this book: 'G' and Pat Kitchener
at Old Barn Nurseries, Dial Post, Horsham;
Mike and Wendy Yendell of Aristaquatics,
Billingshurst; Stuart Thraves at Blagdon,
Bridgwater; Murrells Nursery, Pulborough;
Gardens etc, Washington; Southdowns
Ornaments for loan of the fountain statue;
and Belinda at Forest Lodge Garden Centre,
Farnham for loan of a terrarium.

contents

introduction

The use of water in the home and garden for decorative purposes is one of the most popular recent innovations. With the advent of compact equipment, particularly submersible pumps, and the imaginative use of modern materials, water gardening in all its forms has become easy to try. This particularly applies to the use of water indoors.

Until recent years water was rarely encountered in the ordinary home as a decorative element. An occasional pool could be found in a conservatory adorned with a lotus or papyrus, or perhaps a tropical waterlily, but other than that water was not commonly used. The growth in its popularity has resulted from the development of compact, self-contained moving water features. Table-top and wall fountains are now available in garden centres in rich diversity and are used not only in the home, but in the office and workplace as well.

The sound of moving water is therapeutic and the additional humidity provided by its presence is generally beneficial to the home environment. In circumstances where it is possible to grow aquatic plants, these can make a bold show, the natives of the tropics for the most part being far more exotic and sophisticated than their temperate counterparts, especially the deep-water and marginal species and varieties. Using water indoors and growing plants requires similar skills to caring for a traditional outdoor pool successfully. However, light and temperature are more critical, for to maintain an all-year-

round display of aquatics, the light must be of high quality and the water temperature warm and consistent. Rather surprisingly a number of usually terrestrial indoor plants adapt to aquatic cultivation, particularly amongst those varieties that are frequently grown as houseplants. This opens up a whole range of opportunities for the enthusiastic gardener, for although one or two species have been grown in aquariums for many years, a whole range of others are proving equally as versatile.

In addition to true water gardens, where a pool is the main component, planted aquariums offer the water gardener the chance of growing a wide range of aquatic plants indoors. Traditionally the preserve of the fishkeeper, these can be transformed into leafy underwater landscapes and are especially valuable where space is limited. Not only can natural plantings be arranged, but underwater 'pictures' produced utilizing both man-made and natural decorations.

Terrariums and bottle gardens are on the fringes of aquaculture, but are often linked to it, or become part of the aquatic scene. The same is true of insectivorous plant culture, for these little gems are naturally plants of swamps and marshes. If you want a decorative indoor water feature without a main component of plants or moving water, then consider a floating garden. Either with or without plants, the opportunities for enjoying water indoors are legion.

Above: A traditional style wall fountain is easily installed and can bring moving
water successfully indoors without requiring too much space.
Right: Many modern moving water features are of extremely imaginative design
and make use of the latest materials and technology to excellent effect.

raised conservatory pools

Water can add a new and exciting dimension to a conservatory. Not only can a wide range of interesting aquatic plants be cultivated, but the sound of moving water can be added to the ambience together with that delightful atmosphere which comes when water, plants and warmth associate together.

The great benefit of a raised pool is that it can be easily added after the conservatory's construction and by being above ground level it is more easily enjoyed. Thoughtful design can ensure that provision is made for sitting on the edge of the pool and enjoying the fish and plants at close quarters. There is nothing quite as therapeutic after a stressful day at work.

The addition of a fountain can change the whole feel of the conservatory, effectively serving as a humidifier and greatly improving the atmosphere for other plants. However, it does restrict the variety of plants that can

Below: A large indoor pool can be planted very like an outdoor pond with a reasonable expectation of achieving a natural eco-balance.

Above: *A raised pool is more easily enjoyed. The tiled surround allows you to sit on the edge and observe the fish and plants closely.*

Left: *Water does not have to be planted traditionally in order to be enjoyed. Here moving water falling into a small raised pool, without plants or fish, creates an attractive feature in a very modern setting.*

be used, for tropical waterlilies, surface-floating aquatics and, to a lesser degree, lotus dislike moving water and do not prosper in its presence.

On the other hand a fountain playing over an open water surface with an attractive spray pattern can be beautiful on its own. When illuminated from beneath with underwater lighting it produces a quite magical effect. Indeed, for the conservatory that is used essentially as extra living space, the moving water feature uncluttered by planting is to be preferred.

indoor sunken pools

Creating a sunken pool indoors is an enterprise that requires careful thought especially when it is to be constructed within an existing building rather than as part of a new fabrication. Removal of the soil will cause considerable disruption and also there may be problems caused by creating a drainage system for the pool if this is to be done other than by siphoning.

However, setting aside these considerations, it has to be said that there is little more beautiful than a sunken indoor pool graced by tropical plants and alive with colourful fancy goldfish. Unlike a raised pool, a sunken arrangement does not create a visual obstruction in what is often a limited space. Apart from the labour of excavation which will be considerable, such a pool can be constructed very economically, a conventional pool liner being quite adequate in most cases.

Below: Sunken pools contribute to the illusion of space, for they cause no visual obstruction. Here the plantings enhance the garden scene and protect the unwary who unexpectedly come upon the pool.

Left: *This sunken pool creates an illusion of space, and provides pleasing reflections. Such pools look particularly effective when the surrounding plants are lit from beneath.*

Below: *The secret of success with this pool is water clarity. Of all indoor pools, those holding clear water are perhaps surprisingly the most time-consuming to maintain.*

The establishment of a sunken pool offers you probably the most balanced environment of any indoor feature. Therefore provision should be made for a diversity of aquatic plants. Waterlilies and lotus require deeper areas of water in which submerged aquatics also prosper. Marginal shelves or the provision of shallow areas for waterside and marginal aquatics is also essential. The technique of planting an indoor sunken pool is much the same as for an outdoor water garden, the use of aquatic planting baskets and composts being essential if the plants are to be properly controlled and the pool easily maintained.

conservatory pot fountains

While a fountain is often considered by most newcomers to water gardening as simply a jet of spray soaring heavenwards, or a tumbling liquid sculpture, in modern times it has taken on other forms, most popularly as a small jet or bubbler in a pot.

Now very fashionable, these recent innovations have been brought about by the introduction of improved pumps in tiny sizes. They seem certain to be enduring features on the water gardening scene. They offer the gardener with very little indoor space a wonderful opportunity to enjoy

Above: *A simple bubbling water feature that can be utilized almost anywhere indoors to add sound and movement to a room.*

Right: *A pot fountain like this, where the submersible pump is positioned within the pot, must be topped up with water regularly.*

Above: *Large stones, coloured pebbles and ground glass are frequently used to dress the top of simple pot fountain arrangements where plants do not form part of the decorative scheme.*

moving water. As the pots are mostly quite small and the bubbling or spouting stream of water relatively strong, there is little prospect of plants prospering. Indeed they are a nuisance in such a confined space and it is better if terrestrial tropical plants are used as an associated arrangement next to the pot.

Totally self-contained pot fountains with an in-built pump and a slender electrical wire escaping from somewhere beneath are usually regarded more as table-top features, although there are some fairly large and sophisticated creations available which look more appropriate on the floor of the conservatory.

The most impressive pot fountains are those that work with a reservoir of water beneath them. Sometimes this demands a small excavation before installation, although a reservoir sited on the ground and disguised by surrounding pots and plants to create an additional feature can comfortably accommodate a pot fountain on top. In such arrangements a submersible pump sits in the reservoir and the water is circulated up through the base of the pot. Water tumbles over the edge of the pot onto a bed of gravel or cobbles, these disguising the surface of the reservoir to which the water returns by the action of gravity.

container water gardens

Container gardening is much in vogue and the wide range of modern materials that are available offer the gardener an enormous range of opportunities for colourful innovation. While perennials, bulbs, bedding plants and – to a limited extent – decorative shrubs have been used to great effect in containers, it is only in recent times that consideration has been given to utilizing them for aquatic and bog garden plants.

There is no reason why such plants should not be used in the same manner as those of bed or border. All that is required is a good aquatic planting compost as a growing medium introduced to a water-tight container. Provided that sufficient room is allowed for topping up with water in order to create wetland conditions, there should be no impediment to their successful cultivation.

Apart from the solitary pygmy waterlily afloat in a small simple container, there are a wealth of opportunities for growing individual colourful aquatics and grouping them together in their containers. In a pond they tend to grow quickly and swamp one another, especially in the confines of a small indoor pool. However, when properly planted and grown as large individual plants, they can live their own lives unrestricted, yet at the same time be positioned in the most pleasing and readily changeable arrangement. Apart from decorative pots, aquatics can be successfully cultivated in more unusual containers and can even occupy a window box to great effect.

Right: *The modern varieties of tropical arum lilies or callas are amongst the finest marginal plants for indoor cultivation. Types such as Zantedeschia 'Neroli' are perfect for growing as individual specimens in containers.*

Right: *There are few finer plants than pygmy waterlilies for individual cultivation in containers indoors in a conservatory or garden room.*

Right: *While the majority of container water gardens support an individual plant or small group of plants arranged neatly within them, they need not necessarily fulfil such a role. Here a small rugged pot with minimal aquatic planting provides a cool area of water in a colourful floral setting. In a well-planted conservatory, such a pool of water can also provide sustenance for the local fauna.*

waterlilies and lotuses indoors

Among the many varieties of waterlilies and lotuses there are a number that are well suited to indoor cultivation. Even if space is restricted, provided that the light is good and there is no water movement they will prosper. It is important to choose with care, for many of the most spectacular varieties must have plenty of room if they are to develop properly.

Choose from the many dwarf and pygmy varieties. With waterlilies you need not confine selection to truly tender kinds – some of the pygmy hardy varieties can be used as well. The canary yellow *Nymphaea* 'Pygmaea Helvola' and bright red *N.* 'Pygmaea Rubra' adapt well to indoor life and are especially pretty when grown as specimens in a small container. They will not tolerate tropical conditions, but a temperature between 22°C and 28°C (72-82°F) will suit them well.

There are many lovely dwarf-growing tropical and sub-tropical waterlilies such as *N.* 'Daubenyana' and *N.* 'Margaret Mary' which will grow in higher temperatures if necessary, but they must all have plenty of light. Even those varieties which are night-blooming must receive sufficient light during the day time if they are to prosper.

The same applies to the smaller grown lotuses or *Nelumbo*. These are much more versatile than waterlilies in that they will happily live in a variety of depths of water from saturated compost up to 30cm (12in) of water, but again adequate light is important.

Right: *Of all the tropical aquatics, it is the lotus or Nelumbo that catches the imagination of the indoor water gardener. Although tolerating cold winter conditions outdoors in climates where the summers are long and hot, in most temperate conditions the lotus is essentially an indoor plant and a priority for water gardeners. There are many varieties, all easily grown indoors.*

Left: *Dwarf lotus are easily grown as individual plants in a pot or container. Their long banana-like tubers are planted in early spring and by early summer the container is filled with circular leaves on short, stout, central stems. The beautiful blossoms in white, pink or red are produced in profusion throughout the summer and last well into autumn.*

Far left: *Tropical waterlilies, like 'St.Louis Gold', are magnificent when grown as specimen plants in individual containers. Unlike their hardy counterparts, they are grown from tubers that can be removed and stored in a cool frost-free place in peat or sand for the winter. Tropical waterlilies often have attractive foliage and are available in almost every colour, including blue.*

illuminated features

The indoor water garden offers great opportunities for the imaginative use of illumination. A controlled environment indoors not only permits the creation of great effects using coloured and moving lights, but also allows you to use candles without the problem of a gust of wind blowing them out.

It may seem rather strange to associate candles with water, but some of the prettiest features embrace the use of floating candles. These are now widely available, often shaped and sculpted like waterlilies in an array of colours,

Right: *The use of clever illumination adds enormously to the enjoyment of an indoor water feature. Here the pool has been lit from below with white underwater lighting. Feature stones and plants have been highlighted with carefully positioned uplighters. It is important to make provision for such lighting during the planning and construction stages of the feature.*

Left: *This whole arrangement depends for its visual success upon the correct placement of lights and the clever illumination of plants and water. Everything from the pots, plants and water to the stones and painted wooden flooring must be kept neat and minimalist for the ensemble to work successfully.*

Right: *Without artificial illumination this simple, formal indoor feature would not look as bright and appealing as it does. Careful lighting brings everything to life, and picks out the moving water from the wall fountain as well as the neatly manicured shrubs.*

and frequently producing an aromatic fragrance. Certainly for an evening dinner party or similar social occasion the use of floating candles should be considered, as they produce an atmosphere that is difficult to achieve with electric lighting.

Conventional lighting can also be very effective. White lighting is the most versatile, but special moods and themes can be created by using subtle colours. Soft blues and mauves are particularly lovely. Lighting beneath the water can produce wonderful illusions, as can the use of carefully positioned mirrors to create reflections.

Underwater electrical lighting is safe, but it is still important that all the installation instructions are followed correctly. Modern lighting systems use a transformer which steps down the voltage of the power so reducing the hazards of combining electricity with water. Lighting units are so well sealed that it is almost impossible for problems to arise, but there should always be a healthy respect for electricity where used in association with water. The use of waterproof connectors and circuit breakers or RCDs (residual current devices) that cut off the power supply in the event of a short-circuit is vital.

small indoor fountains

When space is limited, especially where moving water is desired indoors, wall fountains should be considered. It is possible to bring the magic of moving water indoors irrespective of space constraints by using such a feature. An individual wall fountain can be readily constructed from materials that are available from the garden centre, or alternatively a custom-made wall fountain can be purchased, sited and connected to the electricity supply.

Wall fountains are available in a wide range of configurations, but those that are purchased as self-contained units comprise a reservoir and a small submersible pump which circulates the water. Evaporation occurs quite readily and so daily maintenance of the feature by topping up the water is essential. Most aquatic plants dislike moving water and given the limited

Above: *A simple wall mask is very versatile indoor feature, not taking up too much space and providing a generous flow of water*

Left: *A group of bubblers can create a great effect. They operate from a submersible pump hidden in a reservoir beneath the gravel.*

opportunities for their cultivation within a wall fountain feature, they are usually excluded. However, plants positioned around such a feature, usually growing in pots, can greatly enhance the overall effect.

Some wall fountains are also accompanied by a separate basal reservoir pool, the water being carried up through a pipe either chased into the plaster of the wall or threaded through the space in a cavity wall. An outlet is contrived to spout from a wall mask or gargoyle and tumble into a pool below. In such circumstances a small group of marginal plants in the basal pool can be recommended and, if the water is of sufficient depth, a fancy goldfish or two can be accommodated.

Apart from wall fountains consideration should also be given to table-top features. These are usually self-contained

Right: *This is an ambitious wall fountain but the regular symmetry of the fountain aperture and the reservoir canal below enables the water to be precisely channelled.*

fountains sited in a small bowl or container in which a miniature pump circulates water over decorative stones, shells or coloured glass chippings. These are often dressed with artificial foliage. Other styles of containers, sporting copper leaves in a cascade arrangement or a series of metallic scallops tumbling water from one to the other, are also popular. These innovative decorative items are generally positioned as a focal point on a table or sideboard.

terrariums and bottle gardens

Terrariums and bottle gardens resemble garden ponds in that they are almost self-sustaining environments. Large ponds, both indoors and out, are capable of becoming completely balanced worlds where the various elements which complement and depend upon one another work in harmony. As the feature becomes smaller, however, the likelihood of total sustainability and successful interdependence diminishes.

This fact is also true of terrariums and bottle gardens, even where moisture-loving and wetland species are grown. The smaller the container, the less likely it is to be sustainable, but this need not detract from its beauty and with a little ingenuity this deficiency can be turned to advantage. All considerations of ecological balance can be ignored and strong visual elements can be introduced without constraint.

Terrariums and bottle gardens are intended to reflect miniature tropical worlds. They are steamy swamp and jungle vignettes glimpsed through a glass container or aquarium wall. The container itself can be as important as the tropical scene within. It can create a traditional

Below: This bottle garden has an opening at one end, a distinct advantage for air circulation and the reduction of condensation.

atmospheric Victorian feel or an elaborate modern focal point. The choice of plants is endless, for when long-term sustainability is side-lined and the overall picture becomes the priority, a rich tropical atmosphere can be created.

Regular maintenance is important, especially where plants are crowded. Although a high level of moisture is required, it should be remembered that there is no easy way of escape for any excess water. Even plants from marshes and streamsides that are traditionally moisture-lovers do not relish sitting in confined swampy conditions in a richly organic compost.

Above and left: *This terrarium and unusually shaped bottle garden show how beautifully a planted microcosm can be introduced into a conservatory or sunroom.*

aquariums for aquatic plants

Most of us regard an aquarium as a setting for the enjoyment of decorative fish. The plants are a pleasing, but relatively unimportant element, except perhaps as a background or a source of food and cover for the fish. This is reflected in the names of aquarium plants when purchased from the garden centre or aquatic supplier. Rarely are specific names used. Often they categorized under a collective name that can be as general as milfoils or pond weed. They are treated as a necessary, but much maligned, accessory. Fish on the other hand are very specifically addressed by name, even down to individually coloured fancy varieties.

Below: Often aquarium plants are overlooked when an indoor water feature is considered. Aquariums are not just for fish; very beautiful plantings can be made where there are no fish present.

With the popularity of smaller water features and an ever-increasing thirst for innovative indoor aquatic creations, the whole role of aquariums is being reviewed and aquarium plants are being afforded more attention. It has been realized that among the wealth of submerged sub-tropical and tropical aquatics, there are species and varieties that can co-exist happily together in an aquarium feature where the occasional fish can be tolerated, but where the underwater picture is predominantly created by plants.

There are some wonderful aquarium plants available. Individual varieties that are so eye-catching that they will turn the head of the most sceptical interior artist. The marvellous Madagascar lace plant, *Aponogeton fenestralis*, with its lattice-work leaves is spectacular when back-lit in an aquarium, while the rich colours of the foliage of the trumpet plants or cryptocorynes, and the striking leaves of the alternantheras produce an underwater tropical extravaganza which is difficult to surpass.

Left: *As with the outdoor pool where fish and plants live harmoniously together and create a balanced eco-system, so a similar happy arrangement can be achieved indoors. This is a contained world where plants, fish and other aquatic creatures live together, each depending upon the other for their continued existence. In such an arrangement the plants play a key role, the fish being added sparingly once the plants have become established.*

indoor aquascapes

While the use of submerged tropical aquatic plants in an aquarium uncluttered by fish produces a pleasing leafy and tropical focal point in home or conservatory, the creation of an aquascape provides an opportunity for going a stage further and producing an underwater picture or tableau.

Garden centres and specialist aquatic shops now sell myriad ornaments for the aquarium, from the sunken castle and galleon of goldfish bowls to elaborate colonnades, statuary and coloured rocks and coral, as well as colourfully printed dioramas that can be attached to the back wall of the tank for an instant effect. There are as many opportunities within the aquarium for creating an appealing aquascape as there are in the garden of producing a beautiful landscape.

While purists will prefer the use of natural materials such as rocks, stones and bog oak arranged tastefully with associated plantings, the free-thinking can produce a rich diversity of aquascapes from miniature sunken worlds to outlandish modern designs.

There are no rules where aquascapes are concerned, other than the provision of a suitable growing medium and adequate light where plants are to form an important part of the arrangement. If fish are to be introduced, then it is important that there are no artefacts included that could cause unseen pollution of the water. The most harmful of these is copper, which, although beautiful, can be toxic to fish and lead to their death. Otherwise, the boundaries for exciting and innovative creations are restricted only by the imagination of the aquascape's creator.

pumps and equipment

Most indoor water features depend upon a pump for their success. Nowadays submersible pumps are so neat and compact that they take up little room and only need connection to the electricity supply to be fully functional. It is the modern submersible pump which has really revolutionized indoor water gardening.

To create a feature incorporating moving water a submersible pump is essential. This can also be connected to a simple filtration system in an indoor pool. With an aquarium other options are available which utilize an air pump which operates a filtration system, the pump sometimes being outside the tank. Either system works well for the filtration of debris from the water, the air pump also being a primary supplier of air to oxygenate the water which is important when fish are present in quantity.

The selection of a submersible pump for an indoor water feature should depend primarily upon the flow of water required and then upon its size and configuration. This latter is important when a very modestly sized feature is being contemplated, although with the tiniest table-top water features a small pump is often integrated in some way into the container itself.

Filtration systems vary from simple attachments to a pump which take larger suspended debris from the water to undergravel filters which occupy the entire floor of the aquarium beneath the gravel and work on a biological system whereby the debris excreted by fish is trapped and broken down naturally by beneficial colonies of bacteria.

AN AQUARIUM FILTER

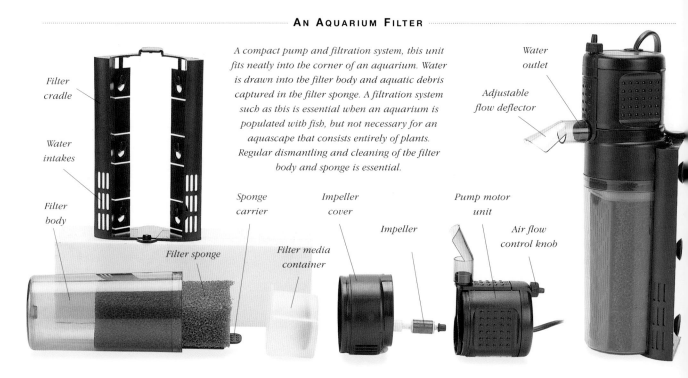

A compact pump and filtration system, this unit fits neatly into the corner of an aquarium. Water is drawn into the filter body and aquatic debris captured in the filter sponge. A filtration system such as this is essential when an aquarium is populated with fish, but not necessary for an aquascape that consists entirely of plants. Regular dismantling and cleaning of the filter body and sponge is essential.

Filter cradle

Water intakes

Filter body

Filter sponge

Sponge carrier

Filter media container

Impeller cover

Impeller

Pump motor unit

Air flow control knob

Water outlet

Adjustable flow deflector

Above: *When selecting a pump ensure that it is powerful enough to lift the required volume of water to the required height.*

Left: *Fogger units are extremely useful for creating a mysterious effect. Take care, however, they do splash.*

Right: *Components such as these pumps, light and fogger unit help to bring indoor water features to life.*

Fogger unit

Combined pump and light

Submersible pump

plants for indoor features

There are many excellent decorative aquatic plants for the indoor water garden, from tropical waterlilies and lotuses to arum lilies and water hyacinths. Each has much to offer, although limitations of space usually mean that they cannot be grown in such diversity as hardy aquatics in an outdoor pool. The majority of indoor pools are much smaller than their outdoor equivalents and other water features have limitations of space which mean that only selected specimens can be grown if the best effect is to be achieved.

Waterlilies are a natural choice, not only the more restrained tropical species and varieties, but the hardy pygmy kinds which are also well suited to indoor cultivation. Lotuses are also excellent, particularly the pygmy and rice bowl varieties. All can be grown as part of

a general pool planting, but are best cultivated individually in attractive containers and then arranged in visual harmony.

Marginal and bog garden plants are numerous, a number of varieties, like the callas or arum lilies and the cyperus species, being commonly grown as houseplants. When introduced to truly aquatic conditions in containers, they often produce a more striking display.

Submerged plants are dominated by those popularly grown in the coldwater or tropical aquarium. Many are genuine submerged aquatic plants that can only be cultivated in this manner, but there is also the surprising prospect of growing many popular foliage houseplants completely submerged if they are planted as juvenile plants. An illustrated example of such a planting is shown on pages 56-57.

The diversity of tropical plants available for use with indoor water features is legion. Most garden centres offer a wide range all the year around.

Pilea cadierei

Fittonia *'Purple Anne'*

Selaginella

Asplenium *species*

Polypodium *species*

Calceolaria *hybrid*

Helxine soleirolii

Cyperus
diffusus

Guzmania
lingulata

Spathiphyllum
hybrid

Chamaedorea
elegans

Scindapsus
variegatus

Dieffenbachia
exotica

*There are many traditional houseplants
that readily adapt themselves to various
roles in an indoor water feature.*

Left: *Aquarium
plants need feeding.
Use a soluble plant
food for aquatic
plants which absorb
minerals through
their leaf surfaces.
Other rooted plants
benefit from slow-
release fertilizer
added to the soil.*

*Lotus and tropical waterlilies are among the most colourful
aquatic plants:* Nelumbo lutea *and* Nymphaea 'King of the Blues'.

installing a conservatory pool and fountain

A pool introduced to a conservatory offers a great opportunity for growing a range of interesting tropical and sub-tropical aquatic plants. If you plan to include a fountain, it is generally not advisable to include aquatic plants in the set-up, but a pleasing arrangement of indoor plants can be used around the pool to create a luxuriant look. It also provides a chance to create an ambience which is difficult to achieve otherwise. The addition of moving water creates a pleasing humid atmosphere and also relaxing sounds and movements. A variety of ornamental fountains – from classical nymphs to modern metal obelisks – are readily available at garden centres nowadays.

Although constructed indoors, the requirements of a conservatory pool are similar to those of the outdoor water garden. These should be modified in the light of what is going to be practical as well as the intended results to be achieved. A number of patio pools are now available in 'flat pack' form which can be constructed at home by any competent DIY enthusiast. These are particularly appropriate for use inside a conservatory. Typically they are supplied as a robust plastic reservoir pool which is concealed by a decorative wooden surround.

If plants are to form an important part either in or as a background to the conservatory pool, then good light is essential. Often the temperature in spring is disproportionately high when compared with the quality of light available and elongated plant growth results. So ensure the best possible light conditions for your plants from the outset.

PRE-FABRICATED POOL CONSTRUCTION

1 *Before assembly, paint the pre-fabricated wooden sections which contain the pool with a suitable preservative. There are many excellent colour shades available.*

2 *Each section is screwed together both top and bottom. It is important to ensure that all the screws are used and that each section is aligned accurately with the next to guarantee a secure structure.*

3 *When half of the structure has been completed, the inner pool section must be inserted. The timber lips that form both the top and the bottom of the framework effectively secure the pool neatly within.*

4 *With the pool complete, provision can be made for a fountain. A level plinth is necessary. This is provided most satisfactorily by two or three layers of clean bricks.*

5 *The pump outflow tube, which is to be attached to the ornament, must be inserted into it and sealed securely. There are many good modern waterproof sealants that will ensure a firm bond.*

Greenery is best provided as an accompaniment to a fountain feature as few true aquatic plants tolerate moving water in such a confined space.

6 *With the ornament in position the pump is connected and placed on the pool floor.*

STONE RAISED POOLS

Left: *This small pool also allows other indoor plants to be enjoyed in its proximity. They benefit from the humidity provided by the presence of water, but create an obstacle to easy pool maintenance.*

Right: *The planters that are incorporated into the structure of this pool wall are independent of the pool itself, but they could be linked to it if so desired.*

bamboo spout fountain

The oriental look is very fashionable now and bamboo looks particularly effective when used to make a fountain in association with simple glazed pottery. There is a wide range of bamboo canes available which can serve as pipes to carry water if the dividing sections between the solid leaf nodes or joints are cut or drilled through to permit the water to flow along the length of the bamboo cane. In many cases the distances between the leaf joints are sufficiently long that you can establish a suitable up-stand or spout without the need for drilling.

A most attractive simple indoor feature can be created by taking a length of bamboo and splicing in a spout of bamboo of smaller dimensions. The spout should be of sufficient diameter to accommodate a narrow flexible tube that will be attached to a submersible pump. The tube leads from the pump, up through the larger diameter

section of bamboo and fits neatly into the spout. It is ideal if the tube and spout are of roughly the same diameter, but, if not, the tube can be glued into the spout with sealant without it showing.

The upright pipe should be sited next to the small submersible pump and wedged into the pot in a vertical position with large stones. The pump sits neatly on the floor of the pot with large stones placed around it so that it is effectively in a small chamber. Further stones are added and a decorative layer of pebbles included as top dressing. Water is then poured into the pot to a depth that ensures that the pump is completely submerged. The pump circulates the water up through the bamboo and out of the spout back into the pot in a circular flow. Evaporation will lower the water level over time, so check regularly to see if the water needs topping up.

MAKING A BAMBOO SPOUT FOUNTAIN

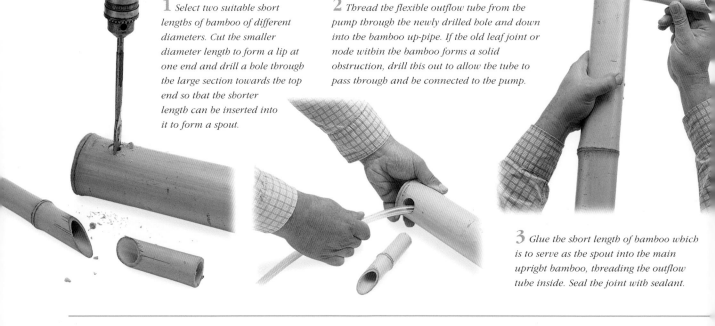

1 *Select two suitable short lengths of bamboo of different diameters. Cut the smaller diameter length to form a lip at one end and drill a hole through the large section towards the top end so that the shorter length can be inserted into it to form a spout.*

2 *Thread the flexible outflow tube from the pump through the newly drilled hole and down into the bamboo up-pipe. If the old leaf joint or node within the bamboo forms a solid obstruction, drill this out to allow the tube to pass through and be connected to the pump.*

3 *Glue the short length of bamboo which is to serve as the spout into the main upright bamboo, threading the outflow tube inside. Seal the joint with sealant.*

4 *Position the bamboo upright in the pot using two or three large stones to wedge it in place. Ensure the outflow tube is not pinched.*

5 *Place the pump on the bottom of the pot and connect it to the outflow tube that runs up inside the bamboo.*

6 *Position a wire support next to the bamboo upright. This wedges into the pot about two thirds of the way up.*

Below: *Here the water flows over the pot and through the cobbles into a reservoir below.*

7 *Place a selection of large polished stones onto the wire support in order to disguise it and so that a water chamber is created for the pump below. The pot is then filled with water to just beneath the level of the stones.*

Left: *The finished fountain will need regular topping up.*

creating an aquatic plant display

One of the best ways of growing tropical and sub-tropical aquatic and marginal plants is in decorative pots. While theoretically they should grow best in a traditional lattice-work aquatic planting basket in aquatic compost, this is only the case in a warm tropical or sub-tropical climate when they are out in the open.

In a conservatory or outdoor room the conditions are not always conducive to successful growth in static water features owing to varying qualities of light and temperature. When plants are grown in pots, however, they can be easily moved around to take advantage of suitable conditions.

Marginal aquatics are particularly well suited to being grown individually in pots and once well established they make a striking feature. Carefully select the pot – it must both be of sufficient size to accommodate the plant, and of an appearance that complements it. Growing a large papyrus in a pot of Arabian appearance, or a canna in a hot-coloured container which reflects the plant's Indian origin, can make all the difference to the overall effect of the planting.

Plants can be grown in pots of the same design, but of varying dimensions, and grouped together for a pleasing effect. Alternatively if your pots are simply functional and of no intrinsic beauty in their own right, then set the arrangement within a larger decorative feature.

Whatever arrangement is decided, all tropical and sub-tropical marginal plants should be grown in an aquatic planting compost and set sufficiently low in the pot so that a couple of centimetres of water can be maintained over the compost surface.

PLANTING A DECORATIVE POT

1 *There are many decorative pots that are suitable for the cultivation of aquatics. The majority have drainage holes which require sealing. The simplest method to make a pot watertight is to use a waterproof sealant and a marble. Put a quantity of sealant in the hole and embed the marble into it.*

2 *Place a generous layer of aquatic planting compost into the bottom of the pot. The new plant will root strongly into this.*

3 *Remove the plant from its pot and place it in position. Ensure that the top of the rootball is several centimetres below the top of the pot to allow for the addition of water.*

Plants Used

Cyperus papyrus/all year round/marginal
Canna hybrids/summer/marginal
Zantedeschia (Calla) hybrids/summer and
   autumn/marginal

Alternative Plants

Cyperus alternifolius/all year round/
   marginal
Thalia dealbata/summer/marginal

Below: *Fine examples of sub-tropical marginal aquatics that adapt readily to container cultivation. From left to right:* Zantedeschia *hybrid,* Cyperus papyrus *and* Canna *hybrid.*

4 *Once further compost has been added and firmed down, top dress the surface with a layer of well-washed pea shingle.*

5 *Add water, soaking the compost. When potting is complete, the plant should be standing in several centimetres of water.*

This wall fountain uses a spider plant or Chlorophytum *for decoration. Not an aquatic plant, it is growing in a sealed pot plunged in the water. Regular repotting is essential.*

planting a window box for bog plants

Window boxes are traditionally positioned beneath a window, suspended on brackets and filled with colourful annuals, biennials, bulbs or herbs. They use a lightweight compost and are mostly completely re-planted twice annually. In recent years, however, there have been changes in conventional thinking regarding the window box, not only in terms of the plants which it might accommodate, but also its role in the garden. Increasingly what was regarded once simply as a window box has metamorphosed into a versatile trough, often planted with subjects of perennial duration.

This trend has resulted in a wide array of window boxes and troughs being manufactured which can accommodate any kind of plant that the imaginative gardener may care to grow. A large number of them have evolved such that they are actually too big successfully to fulfil their original

Right: The popular arum or calla lilies are ideal for window box cultivation. Zantedeschia 'Rubilite Rose' is one of a modern generation of varieties that are widely available from garden centres.

PLANTING A BOG WINDOW BOX

PLANTING SUGGESTIONS

Plants Used

Chamaedorea elegans/all year round/bog

Cyperus diffusus/all year round/bog

Dieffenbachia exotica/all year round/bog

Guzmania lingulata/summer and autumn/ bog

Scindapsus variegatus/all year round/bog

Spathiphyllum hybrid/all year round/bog

Alternative Plants

Acorus gramineus 'Variegatus'/all year round/bog

Zantedeschia (Calla) hybrids/summer and autumn/bog

1 *Ensure any drainage holes in the window box are sealed. Place a layer of gravel in the bottom to a depth of about 2.5cm (1in) and then add aquatic planting compost.*

2 *If an epiphytic moisture-loving plant, like a bromeliad, is to be introduced, a special pocket of peaty organic compost is needed. This should be protected from saturation.*

3 *It is easier to manage special compost provision and the watering of a bromeliad like Guzmania if it is planted to one end.*

4 *Close planting for instant effect is acceptable, as the plants are not allowed to reach maturity. Regular dividing is essential.*

5 *Once the planting is complete, a layer of well-washed pea shingle is spread over the compost. This provides a decorative finish.*

6 *Water thoroughly to settle the compost. Regular watering should ensure that the window box is constantly moist but not waterlogged.*

7 *As bog plants benefit from establishment in a soil-based aquatic compost, a planted window box is more often used as a trough because of its weight. A densely planted arrangement will require regular manicuring and periodic replanting in order to keep it fresh and vibrant.*

function of providing colour at the window ledge, but nevertheless they can make an important contribution to the garden.

With careful selection it is possible to produce an attractive bog garden feature in a window box. Unless it can be placed upon a substantial window ledge, it is unlikely that it can actually be sited beneath a window, for when full of saturated aquatic planting compost such a window box is of considerable weight. However, utilized more as a trough it can be both versatile and attractive, as well as easily maintained within a conservatory or other indoor setting.

growing a pygmy waterlily in a bowl

Pygmy waterlilies are wonderful indoor plants. Although the majority are completely hardy, they adapt well to sub-tropical conditions and are completely at home in a small bowl in the conservatory or living room. Grown alone, there are few more attractive decorative aquatic plants than pygmy waterlilies.

All are of easy cultivation, requiring a generous layer of aquatic planting compost to be spread on the bottom of the pot, and a liberal sprinkling of well-washed pea gravel added over the surface to prevent any escape of the compost into the water.

Water is then poured in and during the growing season it should be regularly topped up to maintain a level near the rim of the pot. Apart from occasionally removing any filamentous algae that seeks to become established, and the regular dead-heading and de-leafing of faded blossoms and foliage, the pot-grown pygmy waterlily is almost entirely self-sustaining.

Of the hardy varieties, the best and most free-flowering is *Nymphaea* 'Pygmaea Helvola', a beautiful canary-yellow-flowered variety with dark olive-green leaves which are splashed and stained with maroon and chocolate.

PLANTING A PYGMY WATERLILY

3 *Cover the surface of the compost evenly with a thin layer of well-washed pea shingle. This helps to prevent compost escaping and discolouring the water.*

1 *Aquatic planting compost should be spread directly on the bottom of the bowl. As much as one third of the depth of the bowl can be filled with compost.*

2 *Take the waterlily and plant it in the compost in the centre of the bowl with just the nose of the crown above compost level. Water the compost in the bowl thoroughly.*

4 *Add water, taking care not to disturb the gravel. Pour it gently onto a square of polythene. Arrange the waterlily foliage evenly over the surface of the water.*

Right: *A pygmy waterlily makes a wonderful centrepiece for a decorative bowl. When grown indoors such waterlilies blossom freely for most of the summer.*

'Pygmaea Rubra' is an excellent red type although not as free-flowering, and 'Pygmaea Alba' is the tiniest white-flowered waterlily. 'Joanne Pring' is pink and not as hardy as the others, while 'Daubenyana' is blue-flowered and sub-tropical.

All the dwarf and pygmy waterlilies are summer-flowering. As autumn approaches and their foliage naturally fades, water can be removed and the plants dried off. Providing that the

Above: *Gardeners who wish to grow a pygmy waterlily in a large bowl or container often find it easier to grow the plant in a proper aquatic planting basket. A small basket enables the plant to be controlled more easily, as the basket can be lifted out for division, repotting or feeding.*

compost does not dry out completely, when water is added the following spring they will return to life, although it is wise to replace their compost annually.

PLANTING SUGGESTIONS
Plants Used
Nymphaea 'Pygmaea Helvola'/summer/ aquatic

Alternative Plants
Nymphaea 'Daubenyana'/summer/aquatic
Nymphaea 'Joanne Pring'/summer/aquatic
Nymphaea 'Pygmaea Alba'/summer/ aquatic
Nymphaea 'Pygmaea Rubra'/summer/ aquatic

planting a bottle garden

The bottle garden is a very practical way of producing a suitable environment for the successful cultivation of a range of attractive tropical plants, amongst them many that are moisture-loving or bog garden subjects. The bottle part of a bottle garden does not necessarily have to be the traditional carboy, a giant spherical bottle that was original intended for the transporting of chemicals. It can be of any shape or size provided that there is room for the plants to develop and a means of gaining access for planting and maintenance.

The glass from which the bottle is made is quite important. It should be clear and unblemished, although a greenish, bronze or bluish coloration can enhance the overall appearance without unduly affecting plant performance. Positioning is important, for while plenty of light is required for the plants to prosper, a bottle garden can become extremely hot if positioned in a sunny window.

While a bottle garden appears to have a chance of becoming a self-sustaining feature, the reality is that it will not. So planting can be more intensive than if a natural environment were being created. However, this does mean that maintenance has to be much more readily attended to if everything is to be kept in good order, and plants will need to be replaced as they fade and die.

PLANTING A BOTTLE GARDEN

1 *Ideally use a soil-based potting compost. Pour this through a funnel made of rolled-up card or newspaper. This helps to prevent dirtying the sides of the bottle. Spread a drainage layer of pea-shingle over the floor of the bottle.*

Gravel

Compost

2 *Spread the compost evenly over the floor of the bottle. View it from the outside to ensure that it is completely level.*

3 *Take the centrepiece plant, in this case* Selaginella martensii, *and plant in the centre of the bottle. Firm gently into the compost.*

4 *Plant the secondary plants, ensuring that they have some room to develop. Create as pleasing an arrangement as possible.*

5 *The planted bottle has a better appearance if the compost is top-dressed with gravel, chippings or, as here, with coloured shell fragments. Remember to water frequently.*

Coloured shell fragments

Above: *This bottle garden has been stoppered so that a completely self-contained eco-system might be established. The drawback to this is the regular flow of condensation down the inside of the glass, which obscures the attractive planting.*

PLANTING SUGGESTIONS

Plants Used

Asplenium spp./all year round/houseplant
Calceolaria hybrids/summer/houseplant
Fittonia 'Purple Anne'/all year round/
  houseplant
Helxine soleirolii/all year round/
  houseplant
Pilea cadierei/all year round/houseplant
Selaginella martensii/all year round/
  houseplant

Alternative Plants

Hypoestes sanguinolenta/all year round/
  houseplant
Ficus pumila/all year round/houseplant

creating a floating candle-lit garden

Attractive indoor water features do not necessarily have to accommodate aquatic plants or moving water. Pleasing arrangements can be made that are not necessarily long lasting, but much more appropriate for dinner parties and similar social events. Indeed, such creations can almost be considered as a type of flower arranging, but one using water as the medium and utilizing a range of natural materials, such as dried fruits and seed pods floating on the surface of a bowl of water. Candles are now available in wide array of styles and designs and many of these are manufactured so that they can float gently upon the surface of the water. Many candles are aromatic and the combination after dark of flickering light and fragrant perfume as they burn is most attractive.

Any suitable container can be used, but one which is shallow and has a large surface area is to be preferred.

If a plant is to be used as a centrepiece, such as the grassy *Scirpus cernuus*, then make sure that the container is deep enough to accommodate the plant pot or basket in which it is growing. This also needs to be thoroughly cleaned before placing it in the arrangement. A small growing plant is especially useful in a floating arrangement as it lends height and visual stability.

Most floating arrangements will have a short life and require replacing regularly. There is always the danger of organic material starting to decompose and pollute the water. However, by using dried materials, this risk is greatly reduced, especially if the water is changed regularly. Remember when using candles that they do pose a fire hazard if left unattended – use them safely and take care if you are using a plant as a centrepiece that it is raised up sufficiently from the surface of the water to avoid being scorched by the candle flames.

⋯ PLANTING SUGGESTIONS ⋯

Plant Used
Scirpus cernuus/all year round/marginal

Alternative Plants
Cyperus alternifolius 'Nanus'/all year round/marginal
Zantedeschia (Calla) 'Godfrey'/summer and autumn/marginal

Left: *A wonderful table centrepiece for the evening. It is important to take heed of the dangers of candle flames, especially if they are in close proximity to plants. After an evening of enjoyment, it will be necessary to empty the water out and to refill the bowl. If any wax has melted into the water, it will have created an oily, unsightly scum.*

MAKING A CANDLE-LIT TABLE CENTREPIECE

1 *Remove the stem and the base of the lotus seed pods neatly with a pair of scissors so that they float evenly.*

2 *To add a touch of colour and sophistication, the seed pods can be decorated with gold or silver spray paint. Allow the paint to dry thoroughly.*

3 *The* Scirpus cernuus *centrepiece plant can often be purchased growing through a tube like this. Tease out the tangled foliage and then cover the surface of the pot with a layer of well-washed pea shingle.*

4 *Invert a clean plant pot into the centre of the bowl. Place the plant in position on top of it. It is now time to add the water.*

Finish off with lighted floating candles.

5 *Place the lotus seed pods evenly around the plant and add other decorative natural materials.*

making a table-top fountain

It is quite possible to create an attractive water feature as the centrepiece of a table or sideboard. However, as moving water is involved there has to be a pump incorporated and so naturally an electrical connection. This will involve a trailing cable and this may be more easily disguised when the fountain is positioned on a sideboard. Remember also that such features can create splashes, so be careful where you site it – it is easy to damage polished or veneered wooden surfaces.

A table-top fountain is usually constructed inside a bowl or container which houses a small submersible pump. The electrical lead for this is generally passed through a hole in the base of the container which is securely sealed with silicone sealant. Alternatively it can be draped over the back of the container and hidden by the display itself. The pump rests on the bottom of the container and may be protected in a small chamber comprising an inverted plant pot, or merely surrounded by substantial stones.

The container is filled with water to within a few centimetres of the top and some form of fountain head contrived which will spout water onto a decorative feature or bubble out of the level surface of a stone as illustrated. The pipe which conducts the water is normally made of clear flexible tubing of the right diameter to slip securely onto the outlet pipe of the pump. If necessary it can be fixed securely with silicone sealant. It is important to fill

CREATING A TABLE-TOP FOUNTAIN

1 *Seal the drainage holes in the base of the pot using a waterproof sealant. Leave this to dry for several hours.*

2 *Drill a hole through a flat stone and pass into it the outlet tube from the pump. Suitable stones are often available pre-drilled from garden centres. Unless the tube fits tightly, it is best sealed in place.*

3 *Put the submersible pump in place and carefully add decorative cobbles. The spaces between the cobbles will form a chamber or reservoir for the pump.*

4 *Position the centrepiece stone carefully. Add water and run the pump so that the flow can be fine-tuned.*

5 *Plants are then added in their pots. Provided that they are not sitting in water, they need not be true aquatics.*

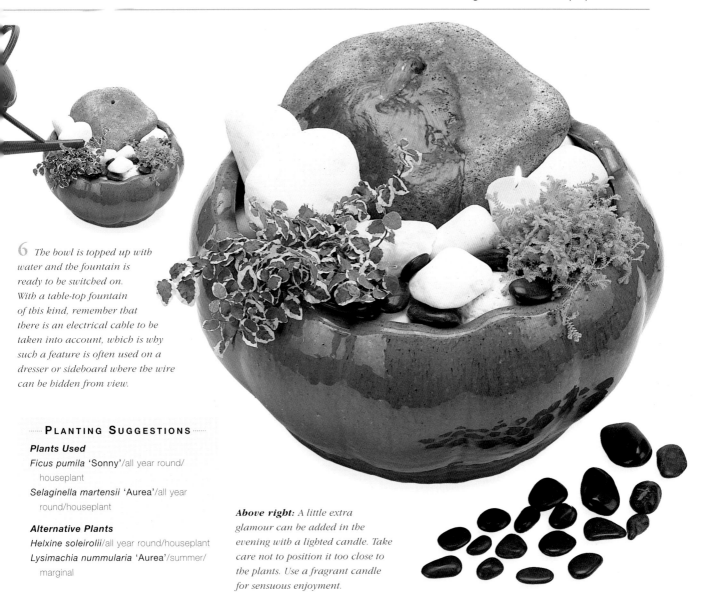

6 *The bowl is topped up with water and the fountain is ready to be switched on. With a table-top fountain of this kind, remember that there is an electrical cable to be taken into account, which is why such a feature is often used on a dresser or sideboard where the wire can be hidden from view.*

PLANTING SUGGESTIONS

Plants Used

Ficus pumila 'Sonny'/all year round/ houseplant

Selaginella martensii 'Aurea'/all year round/houseplant

Alternative Plants

Helxine soleirolii/all year round/houseplant

Lysimachia nummularia 'Aurea'/summer/ marginal

Above right: *A little extra glamour can be added in the evening with a lighted candle. Take care not to position it too close to the plants. Use a fragrant candle for sensuous enjoyment.*

the container with water and to run the pump before all the decorative stones are finally placed in position as it may require some adjusting to ensure that the flow of water is even over the stone. The final top-dressing of decorative stones and pebbles is then applied.

There can be many forms of table-top fountain. Tiny pumps are readily available and merely need positioning within suitable containers filled with rocks, shells, pebbles and glass chippings in varying configurations to create an attractive feature. Indeed it is quite possible to change the components of the fountain regularly as the seasons change or as the mood takes you. The addition of small moisture-loving plants also helps to bring a feature to life and to soften its contours.

planting a terrarium

A terrarium is rather like a small garden created within a greenhouse. The Wardian case of Victorian times which was used as a method of transporting rare and unusual plants from far-flung corners of the globe is typical of the kind of structure that may be used to create a traditional terrarium.

While terrariums frequently feature liberal plantings of a wide range of sub-tropical plants and are often associated with keeping small reptiles and other exotic creatures, some of the finest embrace those plants which naturally inhabit moist places. A terrarium can create a humid atmosphere as well as offer very damp soil conditions for moisture-loving sub-tropical plants.

Although the plants that grow best in a terrarium are moisture-loving, they do not benefit from saturated compost conditions. Constant moisture is much to be preferred. Thoroughly wet compost leads to problems of rotting and the organic matter in it deteriorates quickly and becomes unpleasant and populated by sciarid flies.

Unlike an aquarium or a bottle garden, where plants are often crowded together for effect and maintenance is a frequent requirement, the best terrariums are usually sparingly planted and the plants permitted to grow and develop naturally in the space available to them rather like traditional indoor plants in a conservatory.

PLANTING A TERRARIUM

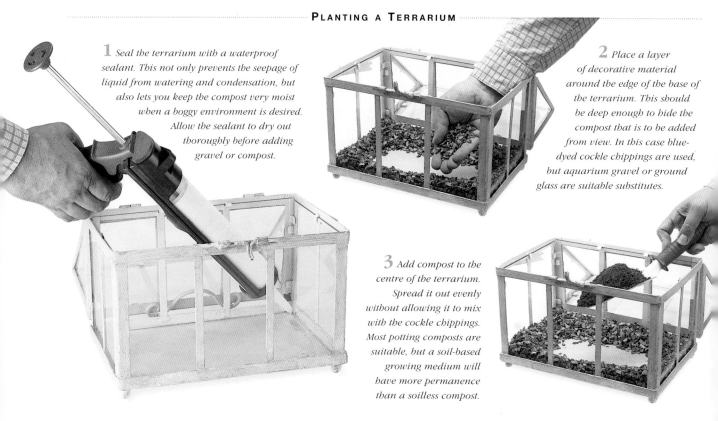

1 *Seal the terrarium with a waterproof sealant. This not only prevents the seepage of liquid from watering and condensation, but also lets you keep the compost very moist when a boggy environment is desired. Allow the sealant to dry out thoroughly before adding gravel or compost.*

2 *Place a layer of decorative material around the edge of the base of the terrarium. This should be deep enough to hide the compost that is to be added from view. In this case blue-dyed cockle chippings are used, but aquarium gravel or ground glass are suitable substitutes.*

3 *Add compost to the centre of the terrarium. Spread it out evenly without allowing it to mix with the cockle chippings. Most potting composts are suitable, but a soil-based growing medium will have more permanence than a soilless compost.*

4 Take the centrepiece plant and arrange it so that it is pleasing when viewed from any angle. Firm it in gently and then add the accompanying plants.

5 Top-dress the compost with a layer of the cockle chippings. Aquarium gravel or ground glass can also be used. The objective is to cover the compost completely.

Below: Although the terrarium can remain closed in order to produce a humid atmosphere, condensation can be reduced if the top is raised to permit air circulation.

6 Water the plants gently from overhead using a watering can with a fine rose. A terrarium will only require watering sparingly after its initial establishment.

····· PLANTING SUGGESTIONS ·····

Plants Used

Codiaeum (Croton) variegatus/all year round/houseplant

Hypoestes hybrid/all year round/houseplant

Pilea cadierei/all year round/houseplant

Spathiphyllum hybrid (dwarf form)/all year round/houseplant

Alternative Plants

Helxine soleirolii/all year round/houseplant

Selaginella martensii 'Aurea'/all year round/houseplant

making an insectivorous plant swamp garden

The vast majority of insectivorous plants originate from swampy areas. There are a number which are epiphytic and cling to moss and debris in the crooks of branches of trees, but the most commonly cultivated species and varieties are native to terrestrial swamps, usually flourishing in peaty or mossy locations.

Part of the reason for insectivorous plants having developed the ability to capture and digest insects is associated with the very poor growing conditions which they have to endure. A wet mossy environment is naturally short of many of the nutrients which plants require. Insectivorous plants correct this by capturing and ingesting insects which yield up the various minerals in which their growing medium is deficient.

It is essential when making an insectivorous plant swamp garden that a very poor growing medium is used. Ideally use one of raw peat mixed with chopped live sphagnum moss. This is the same moss that is popularly sold for hanging baskets. This produces open but wet growing conditions which are perfect for insectivorous plants like *Sarracenia, Darling-tonia* and the *Dionaea* or Venus' fly trap.

In addition to the growing medium being damp, most insectivorous species enjoy a humid atmosphere. When this can be provided by a clear cover such as is illustrated here, they will flourish providing that excessive condensation can be controlled. The provision of vents in the lid of the propagation tray helps to prevent excessive humidity building up.

Above: *Venus' flytrap,* Dionaea muscipula, *is the best-known insectivorous plant. It captures and digests insects in its traps in order to correct nutritional deficiencies.*

MAKING A SWAMP GARDEN

Sphagnum moss   Soilless compost

1 *The best ingredients for a compost mixture are fresh green sphagnum moss and soilless compost, especially low-nutrient seed or cutting compost.*

2 *Chop up the green sphagnum moss and add to it 50 per cent by volume soilless compost and mix thoroughly by hand.*

3 *Place the compost mixture into the watertight tray of a small propagator (seal any drainage holes if necessary) and spread it out to almost the depth of the tray.*

4 *Take the principal plant – here* Sarracenia *– and position it carefully. If the pot ball is too deep for the tray, remove some of the compost from the bottom.*

5 *Arrange the other insectivorous plants, so that there is a little space between them and they are not touching. Firm the compost tightly around the plants.*

6 *Top-dress the tray with green sphagnum moss. Use unchopped moss, as it may well become established and grow naturally if provided with sufficient moisture. This creates an ideal environment for the plants.*

7 *Water the plants thoroughly using a watering can with a fine rose. Replace the lid. For a closed environment shut the ventilators on the top.*

8 *Once established, the garden is sustainable, especially if the moss starts to grow. Although opportunities for capturing insects will be limited, the plants should still prosper.*

PLANTING SUGGESTIONS

Plants Used

Dionaea muscipula/summer/bog
Drosera aliciae/summer/bog
Drosera capensis 'Alba'/summer/bog
Pinguicula moranensis/summer/bog
Sarracenia species/summer/bog

Alternative Plants

Drosera rotundifolia/summer/bog
Pinguicula grandiflora/summer/bog

planting a conservatory aquarium

Aquarium plants can produce a most attractive feature when grown alone and arranged as an underwater garden. There is a rich diversity of submerged aquatic plants with a wide array of foliage shapes, sizes and colours. Among the many popular kinds are not only true aquatics but a number of widely cultivated indoor terrestrial plants which adapt readily to life in an aquarium.

Although theoretically it should be possible to produce a balanced eco-system within an aquarium where only plants are present, this is unlikely if a really attractive display is to be created, for there is considerable maintenance involved in keeping the display in good order and this will necessitate periodic disturbance.

Coldwater plants are more likely to be able to be maintained as a viable eco-system as their growth and development is slower, but it is still likely that the best effect will require your additional help in ensuring water clarity and freedom from filamentous algae. When

PLANTING AN AQUARIUM

1 *Place a layer of aquarium gravel around the edge. This obscures the compost which is added from view.*

2 *Add water carefully. Pour it directly onto a plate placed on the gravel so that the compost beneath is not disturbed.*

3 *Install the combined pump and filter unit. This fits neatly into the corner of the aquarium and can be disguised by planting.*

4 *The aquarium plants are added, as well as decorative bogwood. Lead-weighted plants can be planted into holes in the bogwood.*

5 *With planting complete, fish can be added. Float the bag in the water for several minutes to allow the water temperatures to equalize.*

6 *The pump and filter should now be switched on. This should help to ensure continued crystal clear water.*

choosing plants be sure of the
temperature range at which they are
happiest. Many like vallisneria will
span all the ranges, but others will
sulk under cool conditions, or
conversely become etiolated if
exposed to high temperatures and
moderate light.

Aquarium plants are very easy-going.
Start with small leafy specimens and
ensure that they are planted into a
good planting compost. Take great
care when introducing the plants

*Above: A well-established aquarium, which
makes good used of a wide range of aquarium
plants. This eco-system should be sustainable
with careful attention.*

to remove any snails or snail eggs
as aquatic snails are the greatest
impediment to a successful outcome.
Plants also benefit from the addition
of carbon dioxide to the water as a
fertilizer. Simple systems that can
be fitted to the tank are available
commercially; one such is illustrated
on pages 58-59.

PLANTING SUGGESTIONS

Plants Used

Cryptocoryne sp./all year round/aquatic
Echinodorus paniculatus/all year round/
  aquatic
Egeria densa/all year round/aquatic
Nomophila stricta/all year round/aquatic
Vallisneria spiralis/all year round/aquatic
Vallisneria tortifolia/all year round/aquatic

Alternative Plants

Bacopa monnieri/all year round/aquatic
Hemiographis colorata/all year round/
  aquatic

making an aquascape

An aquascape could be interpreted as a landscape that exists beneath the water. Indoors it is likely to be created in an aquarium or similar glass-sided container, for it is essentially a landscaped picture viewed from the side. It is also mostly in miniature scale and can be naturally contrived or wholly artificial according to your personal taste.

Construction starts with an empty tank and a view must be taken as to the position of major features. These may be rocks, ornaments or specimen plants. As there is limited space it is important that the positions and levels of the focal elements are determined before the rest of aquascape is created. It is also useful to choose a printed background and to fix it in position on the back wall of the tank at this time as it can have a considerable influence upon the positioning of the various key elements. A wide variety of printed backgrounds can be bought 'off the roll' at aquatic and fishkeeping outlets.

When producing an aquascape think of it as a garden both from the construction and maintenance point of view. Ensure that planting positions retain sufficient compost to enable the plants to prosper, and yet at the same time they are accessible for trimming and tidying. The surface covering of gravel or coloured shells should be sufficiently deep to prevent the compost beneath from dirtying the water but not be so deep as to prevent plants from developing properly. Visually open spaces are important and so resist the temptation of crowding the aquascape and making the overall view too busy.

MAKING AN AQUASCAPE

Left: An aquascape is a living aquatic picture, often romantic and fanciful, perhaps decorated with ornaments and a printed background. While it is a combination of fantasy and reality, the plants require the same maintenance regime as those in a normal aquarium.

1 *Select a suitable decorative paper background and cut it exactly to size before gluing it firmly to the outside back wall of the aquarium.*

2 *Add aquarium compost to those areas of the aquarium where planting is intended. Do not run compost close to the glass sides.*

3 *Add decorative aquarium gravel. Pour around the edges to hide the compost and then top-dress the whole base of the tank.*

4 *Place a plate in the centre of the tank and gently run water over this so that the flow does not disturb the gravel and soil.*

5 *Install the filter unit discreetly in the corner of the aquarium so that it can be hidden by planting or ornaments.*

6 *Arrange and plant the most structural aquarium plants first. As the aquascape develops, it should be constantly observed.*

7 *Less important plants can be tucked in behind specimen plants to add depth to the leafy planting. Egeria is a good filler plant.*

PLANTING SUGGESTIONS

Plants Used

Alternanthera roseafolia/all year round/aquatic
Ceratopteris thalictroides/all year round/aquatic
Echinodorus paniculatus/all year round/aquatic
Egeria densa/all year round/aquatic
Hemiographis colorata/all year round/aquatic
Lysimachia nummularia 'Aurea'/all year
   round/aquatic
Nomaphila stricta/all year round/aquatic
Ophiopogon 'Kyoto'/all year round/aquatic

Alternative Plants

Bacopa monnieri/all year round/aquatic
Vallisneria spiralis/all year round/aquatic

8 *Ornaments are added to complete the picture. Apart from static ornaments, it is possible to introduce moving ones, which attach to a pump airline. An aquascape requires regular maintenance in order to retain its quality. Regular de-leafing of the faded foliage of aquarium plants, together with the periodic scraping of the inside of the glass to prevent algae build-up, are essential.*

growing houseplants underwater

Gardeners who are used to the conventional cultivation of houseplants are often startled by the manner in which many aquarists treat young specimens as submerged aquatics. This goes back many years when orchids like spiranthes and pot plants such as the aluminium plant were utilized as temporary inhabitants of the aquarium. Many different plants were tried and now a complete range of attractive foliage plants are offered as submerged aquatics, often using different popular names.

For traditional gardeners this treatment of young plants may seem like sacrilege, but one has to acknowledge that for some plants, like the colourful leafed alternantheras, it has been their salvation. Widely grown in Victorian and Edwardian times as carpet bedding plants, when this fashion was over they virtually disappeared from cultivation. The discovery that they are among the most colourful and pleasing foliage plants for aquarium cultivation has secured their future, for they are now to be found in garden centres and pet shops everywhere.

Using houseplants as submerged plants requires care in selection. Many, such as *Spathiphyllum*, *Pilea* and *Fittonia*, are known to adapt well to an aquatic lifestyle and these can be introduced successfully as small plants, even if they have previously been growing in the usual terrestrial fashion. Others require gradual adaptation, golden creeping jenny for example being grown as a land plant with the stems trailing first into the water and once adapted to an aquatic life, these being removed and transplanted as an entirely submerged, but very successful, aquatic.

Above: Pilea cadierei *is also known as the aluminium plant because of its silvery marked foliage. A very popular indoor foliage houseplant, it is well adapted to life totally submerged in the aquarium tank.*

HOUSEPLANTS UNDER WATER

1 *Houseplants that have been grown in pots should have some of their compost removed before planting in the gravel and compost substrate.*

2 *Introduce one or two cobbles to vary the terrain. This enables compost to be built up behind them and gives additional height.*

3 *Arrange the planting so that it appears as a balanced picture. Plants like* Spathiphyllum *are ideal as they form neat clumps.*

4 *Further decorations can be added. Here black polished stones are arranged to contrast with the plain white gravel.*

5 *Once planting is complete, the plants should be carefully manicured. This includes the removal of any excessively tall foliage.*

6 *Place the filter unit in position. It fits neatly into the corner of the aquarium and can be disguised by planting.*

7 *Add water, taking care not to disturb the gravel. Allow the water to run gently into a polythene bag, which rests on the gravel.*

8 *As the water level rises, the polythene bag rises with it. The bag remains in position until the aquarium is filled.*

···· PLANTING SUGGESTIONS ····

Plants Used

Dracaena hybrid/all year round/aquatic

Fittonia 'Pink Anne'/all year round/aquatic

Hypoestes hybrid/all year round/aquatic

Pilea cadierei/all year round/aquatic

Spathiphyllum hybrid (dwarf form)/
  all year round/aquatic

Spathiphyllum wallisii 'Cupido'/all year
  round/aquatic

Alternative Plants

Chamaedorea elegans/all year round/
  aquatic

Chlorophytum elatum 'Variegatum'/
  all year round/aquatic

setting up a carbon dioxide fertilization system

To ensure a vigorous and healthy growth of aquatic plants in an aquarium tank, the installation of a carbon dioxide fertilization system is of enormous benefit. When plant growth is unsatisfactory, especially when lighting is good and the correct growing medium is being used, then the lack of availability of free carbon dioxide is usually the problem. This is an important nutrient in the plants' normal daily functions and a vital element in the process of photosynthesis, and a shortage of it results in poor development and growth.

In a filtered aquarium carbon dioxide deficiency is commonly encountered and it is in such situations that a fertilization installation is likely to be most necessary. In addition to assisting with plant growth, carbon dioxide prevents the precipitation of calcium dissolved in the water thereby reducing its hardness. In order that this form of

calcium should remain in solution and the pH value be stabilized, a quantity of free carbon dioxide is necessary. This can best be supplied by using a simple fertilization system, such as is illustrated.

A typical system consists of a carbon dioxide dispensing chamber which is attached to the side of the planted aquarium and adjusted so that the water outlet is just beneath the surface of the water. This chamber is connected to a carbon dioxide-dispensing can which is used to charge the diffusion bell with a quantity of gas. The system is finely adjusted so that a very slow stream of bubbles is released into the water. Ideally the diffusion chamber should be charged in the morning and then replenished during the day. There is no merit in doing so at night-time as, in the absence of light, the nature of plant respiration changes as they take in oxygen and expel carbon dioxide.

A CARBON DIOXIDE FERTILIZATION SYSTEM

2 The chamber comprising the diffusion bell is secured to the corner of the aquarium by a single clip. Once installed it is quite simple to disguise with planting. It is important that the chamber is submerged.

Install the chamber once the aquarium is full of water.

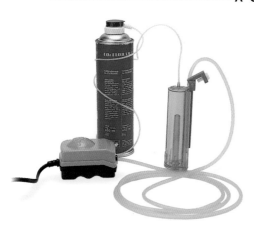

1 A simple carbon dioxide fertilization system consists of an air pump, airline, a diffusion bell and a carbon dioxide gas canister. The system can be purchased complete from most aquatic suppliers.

3 Once the chamber is installed, connect the carbon dioxide dispensing can. Release a little carbon dioxide in order to displace water in the diffusion bell.

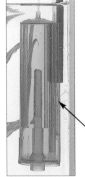

4 *The air pump is connected to the airline. With careful adjustment this allows bubbles of carbon dioxide to be released very slowly into the tank water.*

Carbon dioxide bubbles escape through the outlet tube into the aquarium.

5 *The finished tank with the airpump and carbon dioxide diffusion chamber in position. Bubbles of gas will be released slowly into the water during the day.*

Above: *The use of a carbon dioxide fertilization system ensures that aquatic plants enjoy vigorous and healthy growth. Even though the lighting may be good and a suitable compost is employed, there is no guarantee that aquarium plant growth will be robust and healthy. An infusion of carbon dioxide helps enormously.*

maintaining water clarity

Water management indoors is slightly more difficult than in cooler outdoor conditions. Changes in water clarity, especially those resulting from organic activity are much slower in lower temperatures. In the warm, oxygen also tends to be dissipated more quickly and when fish are involved closer attention has to be paid to ensuring water movement or the introduction of air through an air pump.

The principles for maintaining water clarity are the same whether indoors or out in that the introduction of liberal quantities of submerged aquatic plants assists the mopping up of the mineral salts upon which suspended algae find nourishment. Having a balanced lighting regime and a generous population of submerged aquatic plants ensures that the opportunities for green water are greatly reduced. Indoors in the features described this is an inexact science and so the use of filters is to be recommended for the physical removal of organic life and debris.

Above: *Healthy plants, like this waterlily, Nymphaea 'Daubenyana', develop when the water chemistry and soil conditions are good.*

TESTING THE WATER

1 *Take a sample of 5ml of tank water. This is usual for most tests of this type. On this occasion, a carbonate hardness test is to be conducted, but the procedure is the same for pH tests, as well as other proprietary chemical tests for aquarium water. Carry out the tests every two weeks to check the water chemistry.*

2 *With a carbonate hardness (KH) test one drop of the reagent is added to the 5ml water sample. This turns the water blue.*

3 *Further drops are added until the colour changes to yellow. Multiplying the number of drops used by ten gives the carbonate hardness in mg/litre.*

4 *With a pH test drops of a reagent are added to the water sample causing the water to change colour. This colour is matched against a chart. The greenish coloration here shows the water is slightly alkaline.*

Maintaining water which is in healthy condition generally follows on naturally from physical filtration. Only when fish are present in quantity need there be any serious concern over water quality. For most decorative indoor water features fish are either undesirable or a peripheral interest.

The acidity or alkalinity of the water is only important when the measurement runs to the extremes of the scale. A periodic check with a pH test kit is simple to undertake

Above: Water clarity in indoor water features needs very careful monitoring because of the warmer conditions that generally prevail.

using a system rather like the litmus test of the school laboratory. There are proprietary preparations available to correct any excess either way, although where conditions have gone to one extreme or the other it is usually best to empty the water feature, clean it thoroughly and start again.

looking after the equipment

Fortunately modern water gardening equipment is reasonably maintenance free. Pumps are now completely self-contained and only periodically require attention. Some of the smaller pumps have few components that are accessible. The larger ones that might be used with a fountain in a conservatory pool general pull apart readily and merely require a thorough washing to remove accumulated algae and organic matter.

The same applies to filters, especially in-tank filters which benefit from regular cleaning. Undergravel filters for the most part are best left alone once they are functioning satisfactorily, particularly if plants are established above them.

Aquarium tanks benefit from periodic cleaning with a sponge scraper which can be used to clean deposits of algae off the inside walls of the tank. If you plan to keep fish in your aquarium you should also invest in a gravel cleaner which uses suction to suck muck and food deposits off the gravel floor of the tank where otherwise they would decompose and upset the balance of the water. Inexpensive units are available which, when primed, use a siphon effect to draw off unwanted material.

Left: The efficiency of underwater lighting is greatly improved if it is regularly cleaned and accumulated slimes and algae removed.

Modern lights, like pumps, are now so well made and compact that the units more or less look after themselves. It is important to keep the glass or lens clean on a regular basis as algae tend to deposit an opaque coating quite readily. Where rotating or coloured disc lens are attached to a pump, then regular weekly cleaning is desirable as not only is there a build-up of slime algae on the lenses, but fine filamentous algae becoming entangled in the mechanism as well may gum up the moving parts.

CLEANING AN AQUARIUM FILTER

Left: Disconnect the pump and filter and separate all the parts. Most modern filter assemblies are easily pulled apart. They rapidly accumulate algae and aquatic debris and should be cleaned on a regular basis.

Left: Once dismantled, clean every part of the pump and filter thoroughly using a stiff brush. Do not use a detergent as a residue of this may pollute the aquarium and lead to the death of more sensitive fish.

There are many pieces of equipment that can be used in the maintenance of an aquarium. Pumps, filters and underwater lights require regular maintenance. Other hand equipment is used in the management of the aquarium. Planting sticks, aquarium scrapers and algae brushes are all very important, along with vacuum siphons for cleaning the gravel.

Below left: *A vacuum siphon or aquarium hoover sucks up aquatic debris from the floor of the tank without disturbing the plants.*

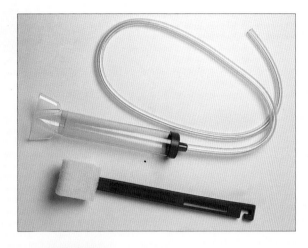

Left: *Two of the most important pieces of equipment for ensuring a clean tank are the vacuum siphon and algae brush.*

Below right: *An algae scraper or brush is used to keep the glass sides of the tank free from a build up of algae. It is effective if used regularly.*

index

Picture Credits
Aqua Press/MP. & C. Piednoir: 5, 24, 25, 26-27, 27, 53, 59. **Eric Crichton:** 3, 8, 16 right (S. Rendell and J. Tavender, Dorset Water Lily Co, RHS Hampton Court 2001), 33 bottom left, 33 bottom right (D. Leigh, Dorset), 43 top right, 50, 61 (D. Leigh, Dorset). **John Glover:** 12 both, 20. **Jerry Harpur:** 1 (Longwood, USA), 4 (Jonathan Wheatman, NYC), 6 (Simon Fraser), 9 bottom (Luciano Giubbilei), 10 (Mark Peter Keane, Kyoto), 11 left (Ray Hudson, Johannesburg), 15 top (Little and Lewis), 15 bottom (Chris Rosmini), 17, 19 right (Luciano Giubbilei). **S. and O. Mathews:** 9 top. **Clive Nichols Garden Pictures:** 7 (Candy Brothers Devt.), 11 right (Newbury Agricultural Society), 13 (Clare Matthews), 18 (Lars Hedstrom), 18-19 (Spidergarden.com, RHS Chelsea 2000), 20-21, 21 (Paul Thompson and Trevyn McDowell), 37 (Lucy Smith), 41 (Godstone Gardeners Club, RHS Chelsea 2000). **Plant Pictures World Wide:** 14-15, 16 left, 31 bottom left and right, 38 top, 56, 60. **Derek St. Romaine Photography:** 29 (Wynniatt-Husey Clarke), 35 bottom right. **Neil Sutherland:** 22, 22-23, 23 right.